Written and illustrated by
Steve Smallman

First published by Parragon in 2008

Parragon
Queen Street House
4 Queen Street
Bath BA1 1HE, UK

Copyright © Parragon Books Ltd 2008

All rights reserved. No part of this publication may be reproduced,
stored in a retrieval system or transmitted, in any form or by any means electronic,
mechanical, photocopying, recording or otherwise, without the prior permission
of the copyright holder.

ISBN 978-1-4075-1289-1
Printed in China

# Little Dragon and the Magic Wagon

**PaRragon**
Bath New York Singapore Hong Kong Cologne Delhi Melbourne

Little Dragon is walking in the sunshine.
Buzzz! go the bees in the flowers.
Tweet! go the birds in the trees.
Squeak! goes the bush …

"Whatever can it be?" wonders Little Dragon.

It's a little pull-along wagon, lying on its side with one wobbly wheel spinning.

"Stay there, I'll get help!" calls Little Dragon.

*Squeak!*

Soon, Little Dragon comes back with his best friends, Prince Pip, and Princess Pippa. They are carrying a long piece of rope.

"What are you doing?" calls Little Baron Boris rudely.

"We are rescuing a squeaking thing!" says Pippa.

"Let me do it!" says Boris, pushing in. "I'm very good at rescuing things!"

Little Dragon thinks that this is a very good idea. Boris doesn't.

They pull the wagon all the way to Little Dragon's cave. Little Dragon gives it a good wash.

Pip straightens the four wobbly wheels.

Pippa paints it blue with yellow spots for luck.

Then, last of all, they squirt some oil onto its squeaky wheels.

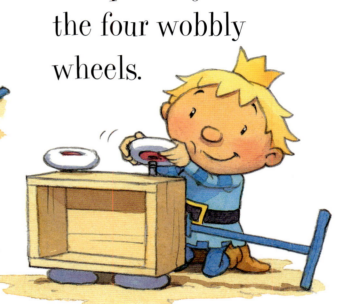

It looks as good as new!

"Oh, Little Dragon," says Pippa, "I wish I had a beautiful little wagon like yours!"

"Me too!" says Pip.

"Oh, but it isn't mine," says Little Dragon sadly, "I just found it and now it's all fixed I'd better take it back again."

Tarum-Tara!

Pip and Pippa hear the dinner time trumpet from the castle on the hill...

...and have to hurry home for dinner.

Little Dragon waves goodbye.

Little Dragon sets off on his own to take the wagon back down the hill. But the little wagon's wheels dig into the ground and it squeaks even louder than before.

Little Dragon pulls...

and pulls...

and pulls! It's very hard work!

Squeak!

Little Dragon sits down on the wagon for a little rest. But the wagon starts to roll down the hill!

Faster and faster it goes, and Little Dragon is a bit scared!

The little wagon steers itself around all the turns, as if by magic!

Wheee! What a great ride!

The little wagon rolls gently to a stop right where Little Dragon had found it. Little Dragon is very sad to say goodbye.

Little Dragon starts to walk wearily back up the hill. He hasn't gone very far when he hears...

"Squeak!"

The little wagon is right behind him!

*Squeak!*

"Are you following me?" says Little Dragon. "Squeak!" goes the magic wagon.

"Don't you want to stay here?" asks Little Dragon. "Squeak!" goes the magic wagon.

"Would you like to come home with me?" asks Little Dragon.
"Squeak, squeak, squeakedy, squeak!" goes the magic wagon.

Which meant, "Yes, please!"

Little Dragon is very tired
and it's a long climb back up to his cave.
So the magic wagon gives him a ride
all the way back home...

. . . to bed.

# The End

Now that you have read the story, join in the fun!

(almost)

Look carefully at the pictures,
then answer the questions:

Who is washing the magic wagon?

How many wheels does Prince Pip fix?

What color spots is Princess Pippa painting?